A SQUIRE ASSISTING A KNIGHT
A TAME FALCON
MIDDLE AGE WEAPONS
the QUEEN of LOVE & BEAUTY
WEAPONS FOR JOUSTING
SHIELD
HORSE
LANCE
CHAIN MAIL
I NOW DUB YOU KNIGHT
KNIGHT
ARMOR
GOBLET
CROSSBOW
KING
KNIGHT
¡CHARGE!
WHEEL PLOW
WANTED
"EVIL IVAN"
THE MOST TERRIBLE WARRIOR KNIGHT OF THE MIDDLE AGES!
TRADE

The Middle Ages
Knights
&
Castles

By
Jane Pofahl

Illustrated By
Julie Anderson

Cover Illustration By
Mark Anthony

Publishers
T.S. Denison & Company, Inc.
Minneapolis, Minnesota 55431

T.S. Denison and Company, Inc.

Standard Book Number: 513-02192-2
The Middle Ages—Knights & Castles

9601 Newton Avenue South
Minneapolis, Minnesota 55431

Introduction

History is the living record of the human race—exciting as it is varied. *The Time Traveler Series* will aid you as you teach the colorful history of the Renaissance and Middle Ages to your children and explore such topics as social structure, medieval government, culture and art forms, scientific discoveries, and the historic personalities who helped shape our own present-day culture.

After each topic is presented, activity pages are provided for your children to implement suggested vocabulary, conduct further research, and provide creative answers/solutions to historical situations. Fun reproducible pages are also included to review the historical and cultural facts studied on the preceding pages.

Each book contains the following:

- topic information pages
- research/activity pages (including maps, charts, research topics, and creative thinking activities)
- reproducible activity pages
- time period stickers

The Time Traveler Series was created to spark the intrigue of your children and lay a foundation for enjoyable history instruction and learning. Have fun!

Table of Contents

Feudalism

After the Roman Empire broke down, Europe was divided into many small kingdoms ruled by different kings. The kings ruled their land with a political system known as feudalism. Three social classes existed during the Middle Ages. The nobility, or upper class, controlled the lands and did all of the fighting. The clergy were the leaders of the Roman Catholic Church: bishops, priests, nuns, and monks. The serfs, or lower class, were peasants who lived on the manors and tilled the soil.

Understanding the feudalistic society of the Middle Ages is easy when it is thought of as a pyramid. At the top of the pyramid was a king. Under him were vassals, or nobles to whom the king gave castles and lands in return for their loyalty and service to him during a war. A powerful noble could be an overlord to less wealthy nobles and have vassals of his own. At the bottom of the pyramid were the poor serfs who farmed the nobles' lands. There were many serfs, some nobles, and few kings.

The kings, counts, dukes, and knights ruled their lands, or fiefs. They supervised the farming on their manors, collected taxes from the serfs, and settled legal disputes between their people. They had to make their laws and not only enforce them, but they also had to protect their own rights.

Feudalism

RESEARCH QUESTIONS

1. In a dictionary, find the following words: *feudalism, nobility, clergy, serf, peasant, manor, till, pyramid, vassal, loyalty, supervise,* and *disputes*. Define each word and use it in a sentence.

2. Make a chart showing the Feudal Pyramid. Draw a large pyramid and show the king at the top, the nobles were under him, the clergy under the nobles, and the serfs at the bottom.

PROJECTS

1. The clothes people wore during the Middle Ages helped to tell others what class they belonged to. Draw a man and a woman from the nobility class, from the clergy, and from the serf class. Label them.

2. You are a reporter for the Serf Sentinel newspaper. You want to interview Lord Loudmouth before he goes to war against his rival, Duke Dunderhead. However, you are only a serf yourself. How are you going to get into Lord Loudmouth's chambers and interview him before he leaves?

3. You are a lord who is in charge of a castle and a manor home. You live in the manor, and the castle is three days' ride away. You receive word that the serfs at the castle are rebelling against paying the taxes you had to set in order to meet YOUR taxes set by your overlord. You feel that you can't leave your manor right now. What will you do?

Manorialism

When a knight (who was also a lord) was not at war, he resided at a manor, which was the center of daily life during the Middle Ages. The manor was made up of all the lands and people that were under one lord. The lord lived in the manor house, which often was a castle. The serfs lived in huts close to the manor house or in the nearby village. During wartime, serfs were offered protection in return for their service to their lord.

The farmlands of the manors were divided into three fields. Each year one field was planted in the spring, another in the fall, and the third was left fallow with nothing planted in it. The serfs left one field fallow to keep the soil from wearing out. They rotated the fallow field every year.

Each field was divided into strips of land. The lord kept the best strips for himself. The church was given at least one strip from each field. The rest of the strips were divided among the serfs of the manor or used as grazing pastures for farm animals.

The serfs did not own the land that was given to them, and they paid taxes to the lord for the use of the land. Since few peasants had money, taxes were often paid with a portion of the crops grown on the land. Serfs could never leave the manor, change jobs, or get married without the permission of the lord.

However, serfs were not slaves. After working the lord's land for two or three days a week, they could spend the rest of the week working on their own lands. If a lord sold his lands, the serfs had the right to continue farming the land under the new lord.

Manorialism

RESEARCH QUESTIONS

1. In a dictionary, find the following words: *reside, service, fallow, rotate, tax, portion,* and *permission*. Define each word and use it in a sentence.

2. What kinds of crops were grown in Europe during the Middle Ages? Find out and draw a chart planning where you would plant crops in your field and what crops you would plant.

3. Many new inventions were developed during the age of manorialism, such as the *horse collar, clearing ax, wheel plow, flail,* and *drop hammer*. Pick one of these inventions and research its uses; then write a paragraph on how this invention improved farming.

PROJECTS

1. You are an artist living in the Middle Ages. A landowner is very proud of his manor and he hires you to draw a picture of his lands, showing which crops are planted in which strips. You will need to make a map key. Remember to include the fallow strips!

2. You are a serf. Your lord demands that you work his lands six days a week. You know that you cannot feed your family by working your own strip only one day a week. What will you do?

3. Would you have liked to have been a serf? Why or why not?

Steps to Knighthood

Becoming a knight was a great honor. Only boys could become knights, and most came from families of nobility. Knights believed in the code of chivalry, which meant they promised to defend the weak, be courteous to all women, be loyal to their king, and serve God at all times.

When a boy was eight years old, he was sent to a neighboring castle where he was trained as a page. He spent much of his time strengthening his body by wrestling and riding horses. He also learned how to fight with a spear and a sword. The lady of the castle taught the page to sing and dance and how to behave in the king's court.

At the age of fifteen or sixteen, a boy became a squire in service to a knight. His duties included dressing the knight in the morning, serving all of the knight's meals, caring for the knight's horse, and cleaning the knights's armor and weapons. He followed the knight to tournaments and assisted his lord on the battlefield. A squire also prepared for battle himself and learned how to handle a sword and lance while wearing forty pounds of armor and riding a horse.

When he was about twenty, a squire could become a knight after proving himself worthy. A lord would agree to knight him in a dubbing ceremony. The night before the ceremony, the squire would fast and pray all night. When morning came, he took a bath to show that he was pure, and he dressed in a white tunic. The outdoor ceremony took place in front of family, friends, and nobility. The squire knelt in front of the lord, who tapped the squire lightly on each shoulder with his sword and proclaimed him a knight. A great feast followed with music and dancing.

Steps to Knighthood

RESEARCH QUESTIONS

1. In a dictionary, find the following words: *nobility, chivalry, defend, courteous, loyal, page, squire, armor, tournament, lance, worthy, dubbing, fast, tunic, ceremony,* and *proclaim.* Define each word and use it in a sentence.

2. Make a chart showing the steps to knighthood. After each step, list duties performed by the "knight-in-training."

3. In order to become a knight, a boy had to practice his battle skills on horseback. One of the exercises he practiced was to joust the *quintain.* Find out what a quintain was, what it looked like, and how it was used.

PROJECTS

1. Knights wore certain colors of clothing during their knighting ceremony. Find out what the different colors symbolized, then draw a picture of a knight during his knighting and explain what the colors of his clothing mean.

2. Make an official poster listing the requirements for the code of chivalry.

3. You are a squire. Your lord is preparing to go to war with another knight. You know that the battle is hopeless and that your lord will probably get killed. Since you are his squire, you are obligated to follow him onto the battlefield and assist him. You also don't want to die. What will you do?

Steps to Knighthood Crossword

ACROSS:

1. Garment worn by a squire during his knighting ceremony.
4. Island country that was the home of King Arthur and the Knights of the Round Table.
8. War games played by knights on horseback in hand-to-hand combat.
11. Place where the king received visitors, performed ceremonies, and held balls.
12. Name of the ceremony during which a squire becomes a knight.
14. What every knight swore to his king.
15. A noble who has trained and proven himself to be worthy of this title.

DOWN:

2. Code of honor that all true knights followed.
3. The time in history also known as the Middle Ages.
5. To be kind and polite.
6. The first step to becoming a knight.
7. The second step to becoming a knight.
9. Name of the upper class during the Middle Ages.
10. Proving that you deserve an honor—you are ___________.
13. To not eat in order to purify yourself.

Armor and Weapons

A knight could not go into battle unprotected. He depended on his squire to keep his armor and weapons clean and in good working condition.

At first the armor was made out of small metal rings called chain mail. A knight wore a linen shirt and pair of pants as well as heavy woolen pads underneath the metal-ringed tunic. A suit of chain mail could have more than 200,000 rings. However, chain mail was heavy, uncomfortable, and difficult to move in.

As time passed, knights covered their bodies with plates of metal. Plates covered their chests, back, arms, and legs. A bucket-like helmet protected the knight's head and had a hinged metal visor to cover his face. Suits of armor were hot, uncomfortable, and heavy to wear. (A suit of armor weighed between forty and sixty pounds.) Some knights even protected their horses in armor.

A knight also needed a shield to hold in front of himself during battle. Shields were made of either wood or metal. Knights decorated their shields with their family emblem or crest and the family motto.

A knight's main weapon was his sword, which was about thirty-two pounds. It was worn on his left side in a case fastened around his waist. A knife was worn on the knight's right side.

Knights used other weapons in combat as well. A lance was a long spear used in jousts. Metal axes, battle hammers, and maces were also used to defeat the enemy.

Armor and Weapons

RESEARCH QUESTIONS

1. In a dictionary, find the following words: *chain mail, hinged, emblem, crest, motto, combat, jousts, maces,* and *defeat*. Define each word and use it in a sentence.

2. Find out what Middle Age weapons looked like. Look in books to find pictures of a battle ax, a mace, a sword, a spur, a battle hammer, etc. Make a poster using the information and label each weapon.

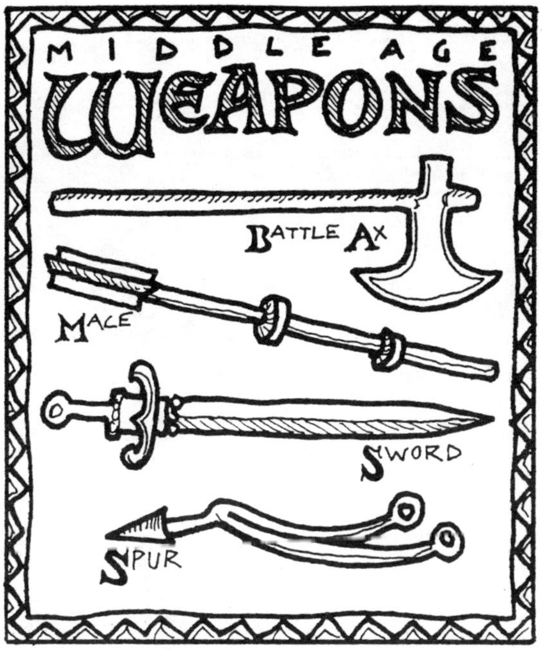

PROJECTS

1. You are a curator in a museum. You are in charge of the Middle Ages exhibit and you have just received a full suit of armor from another museum. However, you don't have enough room for the armor display AND the medieval weapon display AND the medieval costumes display. What will you take out? Why did you choose to remove the display you did?

2. Make a poster of Middle Ages Armor. Draw a suit of chain mail and label its parts. Then draw a suit of armor and label its parts.

3. Make your own medieval weapon. Use cardboard, glue, scissors, tape, paint, and whatever else you need.

Has Anyone Seen My Battle-Ax?

The best-dressed knight would not be caught dead without his proper armor and hand weapons. Help this knight prepare for the Great Tournament of Ravenshire. Dress him in his full suit of armor (found on following page) and attach any weapons he will need in the contest.

Gear for the Great Tournament of Ravenshire

The Castle

Where did knights live? In castles, of course! Actually, castles were never built to serve only as a home for a king or a lord; a castle functioned primarily as a fort for the protection of its residents.

A castle's purpose was to provide defense and offense during wars. Stone castles were built as high as an eight-story building and could be as long as a city street. Many castles were surrounded by a moat filled with water and sharp objects, such as broken glass and rusted metal. To enter the castle, a knight would have to cross a drawbridge over the moat. The drawbridge was connected to the outer wall surrounding the castle, called the bailey. At the end of the drawbridge, built on top of the bailey, was the gatehouse. Before a knight could enter the courtyard, he had to pass through a portcullis, which was a heavy wooden gate. Once he crossed the courtyard, he would ride up to the keep. The keep was where the lord and his family lived and was also the safest part of the castle. A dungeon was built in the basement of the keep, originally for the lord's protection, but later used for prisoners.

Living inside the castle was not very cozy. The castle was cold, drafty, and had few decorations or comfortable furniture. Warmth was provided by fires lit in fireplaces, and tapestries were hung on walls—more for keeping out the cold than for beauty. The castles had few glass windows, so it was dark inside. Servants slept on cold floors, knights slept on tables in the great hall, and only the lord and his lady had their own bedroom in the keep. Instead of changing clothes in a bathroom, people used to change in a small closet-like room called the garderobe. They bathed in a wooden tub of hot water.

The Castle

RESEARCH QUESTIONS

1. In a dictionary, find the following words: *fort, resident, defense, offense, moat, drawbridge, bailey, gatehouse, courtyard, portcullis, keep, dungeon, draft,* and *tapestry.* Define each word and use it in a sentence.

2. Find out about an English castle still in use today; for example, Oxford Castle. Write a report on your findings and draw a floor plan of the castle.

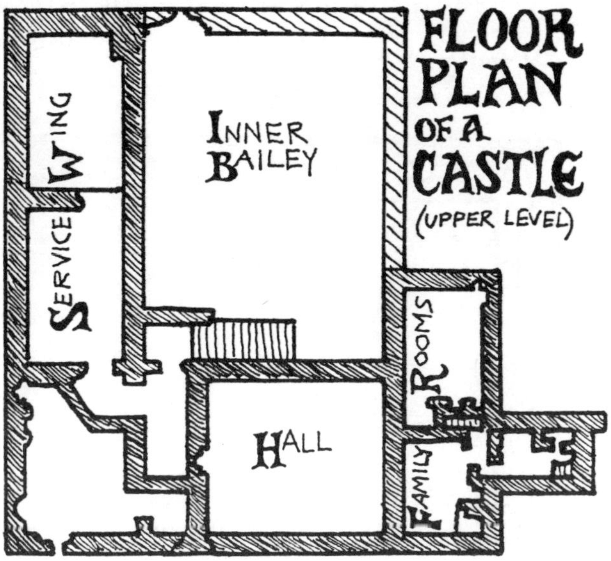

PROJECTS

1. Transform your schoolroom into a castle! Using construction paper and large rolls of colored paper, turn your door into a drawbridge and the walls around the door into the moat. Designate an area for the dungeon. How will you create the keep? Don't forget to make a *standard,* or flag, to fly over your castle!

2. *Tapestries* were hung on the walls of castles for warmth as well as for decoration. Find pictures of famous tapestry designs in books, then draw and color your own design.

3. You are a real estate agent. You need to sell a huge castle before the end of the month, or your boss will fire you. Write a real estate ad for the local newspaper, describing the castle's advantages and features.

Create a Castle

Sir Paysalot asks you, the most celebrated castle architect in the land, to design his latest castle for him. It will be situated on a small hill and you are to add a moat at the base of this hill. Money is no object to Sir Paysalot, so add as many guard towers and turrets as you want.

The Tournament

Since nobles were also knights, they were trained warriors. When they were not at war, knights practiced their skills in tournaments, or war games.

The highlight of castle life, tournaments were attended by the residents of the manor and visitors from neighboring castles. On opening day, noble contestants rode in a procession through the town and displayed their banners and coats-of-arms.

The next day the joust began. A noble maiden was chosen as the tournament's Queen Of Love And Beauty and sat in the judge's stand during the tournament. Two knights on horseback galloped toward each other from opposite ends of a field, each one trying to unseat the other rider with his lance. Knights wore full suits of armor for protection and carried a lance and a shield. If a knight were knocked off his horse, he lost his horse and armor and had to pay a ransom to get them back. The Queen Of Love And Beauty awarded the winner of the joust with a magnificent war-horse or a purse filled with gold. Each day ended with feasting, music, and dancing.

Jousts could be dangerous. The Church tried to make the games safer by introducing rules. There were three kinds of jousts. One version used sharp points on the lances, which could cause death. In another game, knights used blunted lances which usually did not injure opponents. The third kind of contest occurred with real weapons, but the fighting could be stopped at any time. Tournaments not only provided practice for knights and entertainment for the people, but they also gave young knights a chance to gain wealth and recognition.

The Tournament

RESEARCH QUESTIONS

1. In a dictionary, find the following words: *contestant, procession, banner, maiden, ransom, blunt, injure, opponent,* and *recognition*. Define each word and use it in a sentence.

2. Find out more about the weapons used in tournament combat. Write a report on your findings and make a chart illustrating the various weapons.

3. Make a chart listing the kinds of games for jousting tournaments. Under each heading, explain in detail how each game could be played.

PROJECTS

1. You are an artist hired by the tournament's Queen Of Love And Beauty to capture her likeness on paper. Draw and color the Queen Of Love And Beauty wearing her crown at the tournament.

2. Make a puppet show and recreate a jousting tournament.

3. You are a poor knight who just got knocked off of your horse. According to the rules, you must *forfeit*, or give up, your horse and armor, but you don't have enough money to pay the *ransom* to get them back. What will you do?

The Banquet

Meals during the Middle Ages were much simpler than today. Since refrigerators had not been invented and transportation was difficult, people could only eat what they could raise or catch.

A feast held in the great hall of a castle after a celebration, such as a wedding, knighting, or tournament, would be a wondrous sight. A variety of fruits and vegetables grown on the manor would serve as the first course. The main course could include salted beef; fresh fish; a variety of fowl; and tough, chewy pork. The meats were made to taste more interesting (and hide the tastes of rotting) with expensive imported spices. Salt was also a favorite spice, and important nobles and guests were always seated nearest the elaborate saltcellars at the tables. Honey was used from the castles' beehives to sweeten foods.

The lord of the castle and his guests drank milk; wine; and mead, which was a kind of beer. Water had to be boiled before drinking, so most people preferred wine.

The great hall would be set up for the banquet. The lord and other nobles were seated at the head table and used goblets and plates made of gold, silver, or pewter. Less important guests and servants sat at side tables and used wooden goblets and plates called trenchers. Some people used forks, but most used their fingers and needed to dip their hands in finger bowls frequently. During the feast, musicians, female dancers, and comedians entertained the guests.

The Banquet

RESEARCH QUESTIONS

1. In a dictionary, find the following words: *fowl, import, elaborate, saltcellar, mead, prefer, goblets, pewter, trenchers, finger bowl,* and *comedian.* Define each word and use it in a sentence.

2. Find out more about the foods served at a medieval banquet. Report your findings to the class. Illustrate the types of foods as part of your presentation.

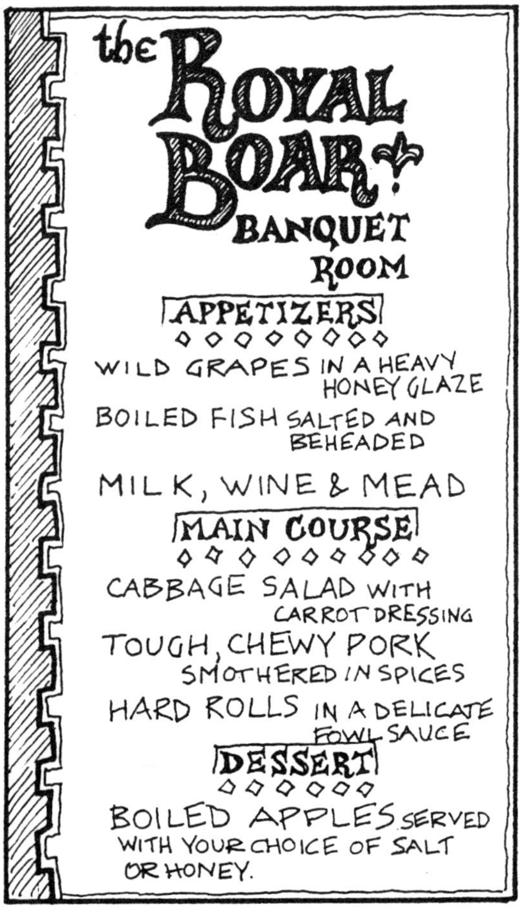

PROJECTS

1. Salt was valued so highly that only those sitting at the lord's table could use it. Design a saltcellar to be used at your lord's next banquet.

2. You are in charge of this evening's banquet. Your lord wants menus for each guest. Create a menu stating the foods that will be served (in the order that they will be presented to the guests).

3. Recreate a medieval banquet. Serve as many authentic foods as possible. Some students will need to be servers, some nobles, and some entertainers.

Falconry and Hunting

Although knights spent much of their time at wars or training for wars, they did take time to relax. Two of their favorite sports were falconry and hunting.

A falcon is an intelligent bird that nobles trained to hunt down and attack other birds in the sky. Female falcons were used instead of males because they were bigger and more ferocious.

A tamer would feed a wild falcon by hand so that it would become familiar with him. The tamer also wore a tough glove so that the bird could perch on his wrist. When it was tame, a bell was tied to the falcon's leg and a hood was put over its head to keep it quiet. A falcon was trained by tying a leash to its other leg and allowing it to fly for short distances. When the bird returned to the tamer's wrist after it was whistled to, the falcon would be rewarded with a bit of raw meat. Soon the falcon would be released from the leash and allowed to hunt by itself. When the falcon killed its prey, the tamer had to remember to reward the bird with food.

Knights also enjoyed hunting wild game. The prey was usually a stag, a doe, or a boar. Hounds were trained to track down the prey by its scent and to obey signals on a horn.

The nobles and their ladies rode on horseback behind the hounds and chased the prey through dense forests and over ditches. A hunt could last for many hours. When the prey was finally caught and killed, a song was played to honor the dying animal. The hunt was followed by a great feast with the freshly-hunted animals as the main course!

Falconry and Hunting

RESEARCH QUESTIONS

1. In a dictionary, find the following words: *falcon, ferocious, prey, stag, doe, boar, scent,* and *dense.* Define each word and use it in a sentence.

2. Find out more about falcons. List three different kinds of falcons and give a short description of each. Include illustrations.

3. The *peregrine falcon,* used in falconry to hunt prey, is an endangered species today. Are all falcons endangered? Make a chart of all the different kinds of endangered falcons and list the reasons why they are endangered.

PROJECTS

1. Present a demonstration to the class on how to tame a falcon.

2. You are a stag. Everything is peaceful and calm around you. Suddenly, you hear a horn in the distance and the barking of hounds. You know that you are in danger. Where will you go? What will you do?

3. You are the court musician. Your lord and lady have just brought down a large boar in a hunt. Compose a poem to honor the noble beast and then set the words to music.

A-Hunting We Will Go!

Help Sir Dillidan find his way through the maze to capture the stag.

Siege the Castle

At the first sign of trouble from a rival lord and his vassals, residents of a castle ran inside the castle walls and women and children headed for the keep. The men of the castle prepared to defend their fortress from a siege or major attack.

Water and oil was boiled in vats, ready to pour on attackers climbing the outer walls. The walls, with high and low places called battlements, provided protection for archers using longbows and crossbows. The most vulnerable part of the castle was the entrance. The drawbridge over the moat could be pulled up flush with the rest of the outer wall. The portcullis was lowered to form another barrier. Many guards were stationed at the guardhouse on the bailey wall with longbows to ward off invaders.

Attacking soldiers used a variety of ways to siege a castle. They climbed the outer walls, tunneled under the walls, and shot at the guards on the bailey with longbows and crossbows. Christians learned how to build mechanical devices, or siege machines, from the Muslims during the Crusades. The catapult was like a giant slingshot and the ballista was a giant crossbow on a platform. Both machines could fling objects far distances and across bailey walls. The battering ram was a large, long tree trunk used for smashing down castle walls.

Nobles were often captured rather than killed. A captive knight could be held for ransom.

Siege the Castle

RESEARCH QUESTIONS

1. In a dictionary, find the following words: *rival, siege, vat, battlements, archer, longbow, crossbow, vulnerable, flush, barrier, device, catapult, ballista, battering ram,* and *captive.* Define each word and use it in a sentence.

2. Find out more about the defense and offense of a medieval castle. Make a chart and list ways to defend and attack a castle.

PROJECTS

1. The ancient Greeks found a way to get into the gates of Troy. They built a gigantic wooden horse and filled its belly with Greek soldiers. Then they wheeled the horse to the gates of Troy and ran away. The Trojans thought that the wooden horse was a gift from the Greeks as a peace offering, so they opened the gates and wheeled the horse into their city. When the Trojans were asleep that night, the Greeks let down rope ladders and climbed out of the horse. The Trojans were taken by surprise, and surrendered to the Greeks. Design a "gift" to surprise a rival lord behind his castle walls and label its secret features.

2. Create a "Wanted" poster for the most terrible warrior knight of the Middle Ages. Draw his picture and include his name, dastardly deeds, and the amount of reward money offered for his capture.

3. Having a fresh supply of food and water in a castle at all times was very important. Why?

Siege the Castle Word Search

S	O	U	Z	T	E	V	J	V	D	E	O	D	S	P	H	Y
F	C	A	T	A	P	U	L	T	C	G	N	C	A	P	F	F
G	F	M	F	B	A	L	L	I	S	T	A	G	C	B	E	I
D	V	C	Y	K	Z	N	P	F	Y	E	W	S	Y	M	V	R
E	B	T	M	V	Q	E	O	X	S	F	B	K	K	C	C	E
V	E	Z	D	D	U	R	R	R	F	X	N	U	U	V	O	D
F	H	Q	K	J	B	A	T	T	E	R	I	N	G	R	A	M
R	Z	Z	I	I	A	B	C	R	O	S	S	B	O	W	R	B
U	J	J	T	U	T	L	U	I	O	H	K	F	P	Y	T	I
C	H	N	O	T	T	E	L	V	S	R	U	N	O	Z	U	V
V	A	S	S	A	L	H	L	A	Z	Q	F	B	K	A	S	B
J	T	K	K	E	E	P	I	L	L	Y	D	F	D	C	N	A
R	A	N	S	O	M	D	S	I	U	L	L	K	E	N	G	H
X	A	T	I	T	E	U	L	A	Q	N	M	J	L	I	Y	O
A	Y	T	E	Q	N	E	J	S	E	S	U	I	J	P	V	I
C	O	A	G	Q	T	B	O	C	B	D	Z	W	D	B	N	L
K	Z	P	E	L	S	T	R	K	P	X	L	L	I	R	P	V

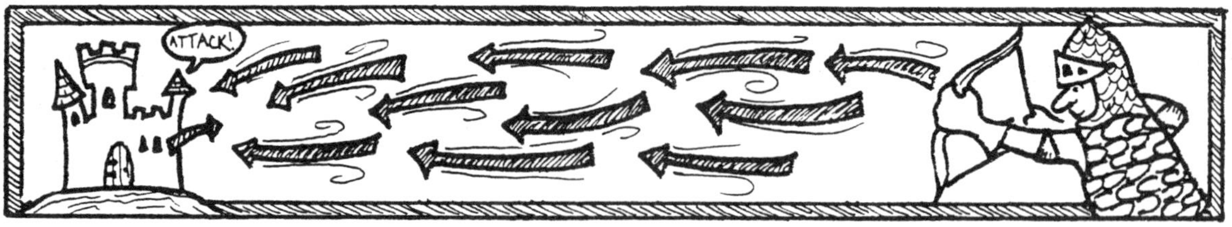

Can you find these words?

BATTERING RAM
VULNERABLE
CROSSBOW
RIVAL
BATTLEMENTS
BALLISTA
RANSOM
SIEGE
PORTCULLIS
CATAPULT
VASSAL
KEEP

The Crusades

During the Middle Ages, a majority of the people living in Europe were Christians. Many nobles traveled to the place where saints were buried and then worshipped there. These trips were called pilgrimages. Perhaps the greatest pilgrimage was to go to Jerusalem, in the Holy Land, where Jesus Christ had lived.

The Muslims living in the Holy Land allowed the Christians to make pilgrimages for hundreds of years. However, in 1071, a different group of Muslims, called the Seljuk Turks, took over the Holy Land and started killing Christian pilgrims.

In 1095, Pope Urban II called a meeting in Clermont, France. He asked Christians to take back the Holy Land from the Muslims. The ensuing holy wars were known as the Crusades.

People joined the Crusades for many reasons. Some felt that it was their Christian duty to God to win the Holy Land from the Muslims. Some fought because they liked adventure and war. Other men agreed to fight in exchange for their freedom from prison. Some joined in the hope of bettering themselves by winning wealth and land from the Turks.

From 1099 to 1291, four major Crusades were fought which lasted for almost two hundred years. The Christians won the first Crusade in 1099, but lost the last three. In 1291, the Christians lost the final battle and went home.

Even though the Crusades failed from a military standpoint, they were important for Europeans. After experiencing Middle Eastern foods, clothing, and ideas, returning Europeans set up major trade systems with Middle Easterners which boosted Europe's economy. The Crusades were also important for their affect on European rulers—since so many nobles were killed in the Crusades, kings took back their fiefs and powerful kingdoms were formed.

The Crusades

RESEARCH QUESTIONS

1. In a dictionary, find the following words: *majority, pilgrimage, pilgrim, ensue, crusade, military, boost,* and *economy*. Define each word and use it in a sentence.

2. The word *crusade* comes from a Latin word. Find out what the word means, and explain why you think the Holy Wars fought for God were called the Crusades.

3. Make a chart listing the reasons why people joined the fighting in the Crusades.

4. Find out more about Pope Urban II. Write a report about his life and how his actions changed the world.

PROJECTS

1. The Christian warriors involved in the Crusades were mainly nobles. Why didn't more serfs fight in the Crusades?

2. Some noble knights brought their entire families along on a crusade. Why would they do that?

3. If you had lived during the Middle Ages, would you have fought in the Crusades? Why or why not?

The Crusades

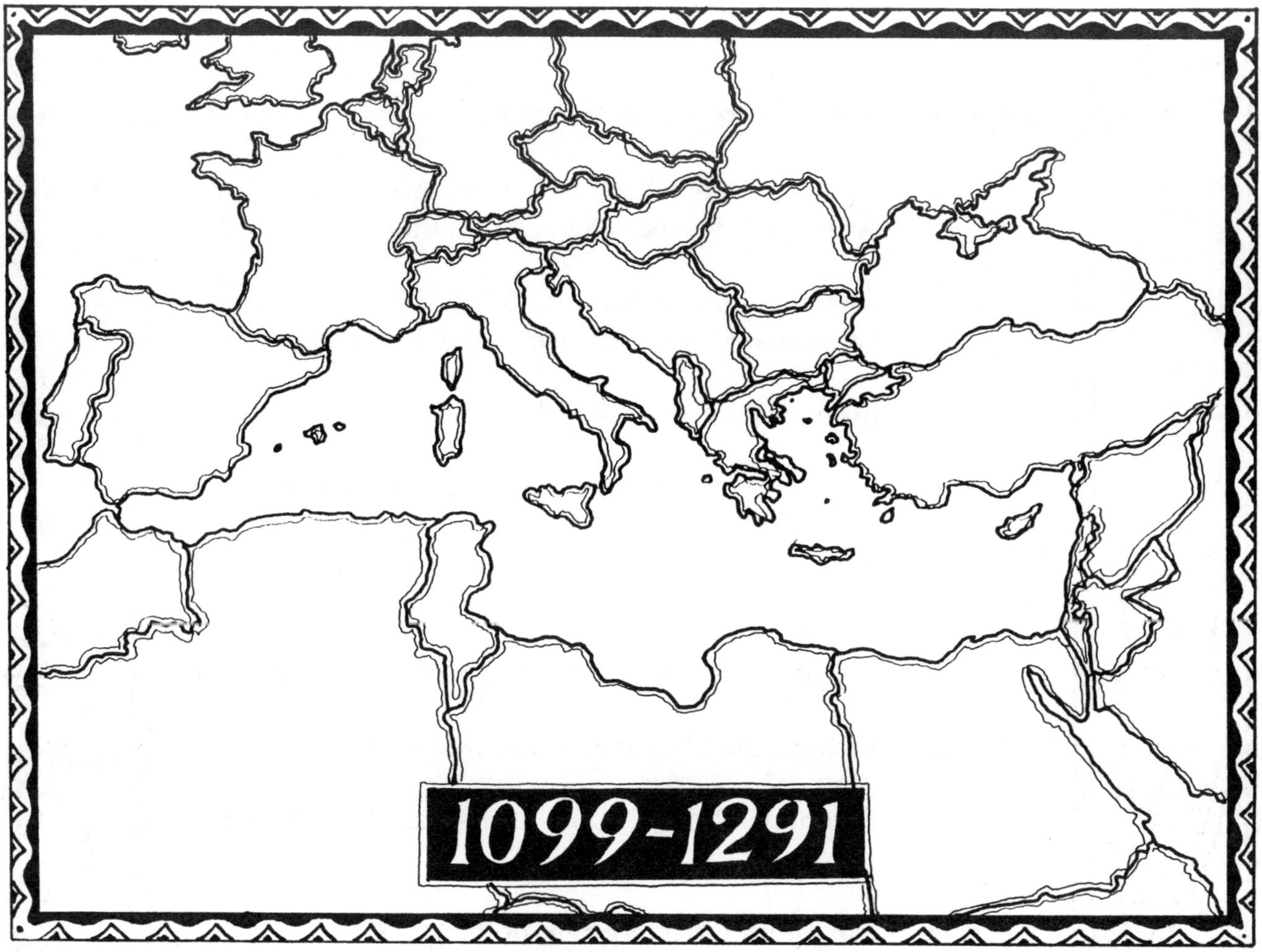

1. Identify the following on your map (refer to a world atlas to find a map of Europe):
   - England
   - France
   - Spain
   - Portugal
   - Germany
   - Italy
   - Hungary
   - Czechoslovakia
   - Switzerland
   - Austria
   - Turkey
   - Syria
   - Israel
   - Poland
   - Bulgaria
   - Romania
   - Egypt
   - Jerusalem
   - Jordan
   - Mediterranean Sea
   - Red Sea
   - Black Sea
2. Color the water blue, the land tan, and the area known as the "Holy Land" purple.
3. Using an encyclopedia, draw the route that Christian knights traveled when going to the Holy Land during the Crusades.
4. Why did the Christians, Muslims, and Jews call Jerusalem the "Holy Land"?

   ____
5. If you were a Crusader from France, would you travel to the Holy Land by land or sea? ______________________ Why? ______________________

   ____

Middle Ages Timeline

455 A.D.	Rome destroyed by Vandals.
500	Western Roman Empire fell to Germanic tribes; King Arthur is believed to have ruled England at this time.
800	Charlemagne crowned "King of the Franks" on Christmas Day; Feudalism began in Western Europe.
1000	Romanesque-style churches first appeared.
late 1000s	Gothic architecture replaced Romanesque in popularity.
1096–1291	The Crusades
1154	Eleanor of Aquitaine married Henry II of England.
1189–1199	Richard the Lionhearted ruled England.
1200s	Roman Catholic Church at the height of its political power.
1215	King John forced to sign the Magna Carta.
1220s	Robert Fitzooth (who is believed to be Robin Hood) lived in Huntington, England.
1224	St. Francis of Assisi received the stigmata near Florence, Italy.
1400	Feudalism on the decline in Western Europe.
1431	Joan of Arc found guilty of witchcraft and executed.
1533	Anne Boleyn became queen of England for approximately one thousand days.
1559	Elizabeth I crowned queen of England.

A SQUIRE ASSISTING A KNIGHT
A TAME FALCON
MIDDLE AGE WEAPONS
BATTLE AX
MACE
SWORD
SPUR
THE QUEEN OF LOVE & BEAUTY
WEAPONS FOR JOUSTING
SHIELD
HORSE
LANCE
CHAIN MAIL
I NOW DUB YOU KNIGHT
KNIGHT
ARMOR
GOBLET
CROSSBOW
KING
CHARGE!
WHEEL PLOW
WANTED
EVIL IVAN
THE MOST TERRIBLE WARRIOR KNIGHT OF THE MIDDLE AGES!
FAIR
TRADE

A SQUIRE ASSISTING A KNIGHT
A TAME FALCON
MIDDLE AGE WEAPONS
BATTLE AX
MACE
SWORD
SPUR
THE QUEEN OF LOVE & BEAUTY
WEAPONS FOR JOUSTING
SHIELD
HORSE
LANCE
CHAIN MAIL
I NOW DUB YOU KNIGHT
KNIGHT
ARMOR
GOBLET
CROSSBOW
KING
CHARGE!
WHEEL PLOW
WANTED
EVIL IVAN
THE MOST TERRIBLE WARRIOR KNIGHT OF THE MIDDLE AGES!
FAIR
TRADE

A SQUIRE ASSISTING A KNIGHT
A TAME FALCON
MIDDLE AGE WEAPONS
BATTLE AX
MACE
SWORD
SPUR
THE QUEEN OF LOVE & BEAUTY
WEAPONS FOR JOUSTING
SHIELD
HORSE
LANCE
CHAIN MAIL
I NOW DUB YOU KNIGHT
KNIGHT
ARMOR
GOBLET
CROSSBOW
KING
CHARGE!
WHEEL PLOW
WANTED
EVIL IVAN
THE MOST TERRIBLE WARRIOR KNIGHT OF THE MIDDLE AGES!
FAIR
TRADE

A SQUIRE ASSISTING A KNIGHT
A TAME FALCON
MIDDLE AGE WEAPONS
BATTLE AX
MACE
SWORD
SPUR
THE QUEEN OF LOVE & BEAUTY
WEAPONS FOR JOUSTING
SHIELD
HORSE
LANCE
CHAIN MAIL
I NOW DUB YOU KNIGHT
KNIGHT
ARMOR
GOBLET
CROSSBOW
KING
CHARGE!
WHEEL PLOW
WANTED
EVIL IVAN
THE MOST TERRIBLE WARRIOR KNIGHT OF THE MIDDLE AGES!
FAIR
TRADE